ECO CARS

Written by
PENNY WORMS

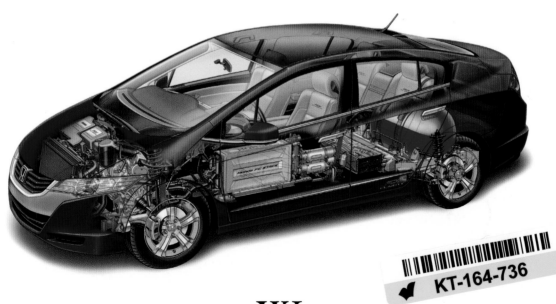

W
FRANKLIN WATTS
LONDON • SYDNEY

This edition published in 2013 by
Franklin Watts
338 Euston Road
London NW1 3BH

Franklin Watts Australia
Level 17/207 Kent Street
Sydney NSW 2000

Series editor: Jeremy Smith
Design: Graham Rich
Cover design: Graham Rich
Picture research: Penny Worms

A CIP catalogue record for this book is available
from the British Library.

ISBN: 978 1 4451 1890 1

Dewey classification: 629.2'22

The author would like to thank Felix Wills and the
following for their kind help and permission to use
images: Jeremy Davey from the Thrust team; Dave
Rowley from the Bloodhound team; and the media
teams at Audi, BMW and McLaren.

Thanks to Felix Wills, Erica Haddon at Toyota UK,
Simon Childs, Nicola Sanderson and The Lightning Car
Company, Richard Gadeselli and the Fiat Group and the
media teams at BMW and Honda.

Picture Credits
AFP/Getty Images: 26/27 main image. BMW Group: 18/19
all images. Corbis Images: 22 centre, 23 left, 24 left. Fiat
Group S.p.A: 24/25 centre, 25 bottom right.
Getty Images: 6/7 main image. Honda: title page and 20,
16/17 bottom, 17 right, 20/21 all images. istock: 23 centre
right. Lightning Car Company Limited: 14/15 all images.
Realimage/Alamy: 16 left. Shutterstock: 6 centre, 22/23
bottom, 26 centre right. Simon Childs (for Lexus/Toyota):
4 and 10. Tesla Motors, Inc: 12/13 all images. Toyota
(GB) Plc: 7 top, 8 left, 8/9, 11 centre and bottom. www.
worldfirstracing.co.uk: 5 and 27 right.

Printed in China

Franklin Watts is a division of Hachette Children's Books,
an Hachette UK company.
www.hachette.co.uk

Disclaimer: Some of the 'Stats and Facts' are
approximations. Others are correct at time of writing,
but will probably change.

CONTENTS

ECO CARS

Eco cars are kinder to the environment and cheaper to run than normal cars. Car makers are spending millions trying to build the ultimate eco car. The reasons are all explained in this book, but the most important for the planet is to reduce **carbon-dioxide (CO_2) emissions**. Carbon dioxide is a gas that is contributing to **global warming**. No one has come up with the ultimate eco car yet, but the new **technology** being developed will change our cars forever.

SUGAR FUEL

Most of today's cars run on petrol or diesel. Both cause pollution. They also come from oil drilled out of the ground. This oil is running out so car makers are trying new fuels to run their cars – including one made from sugar cane!

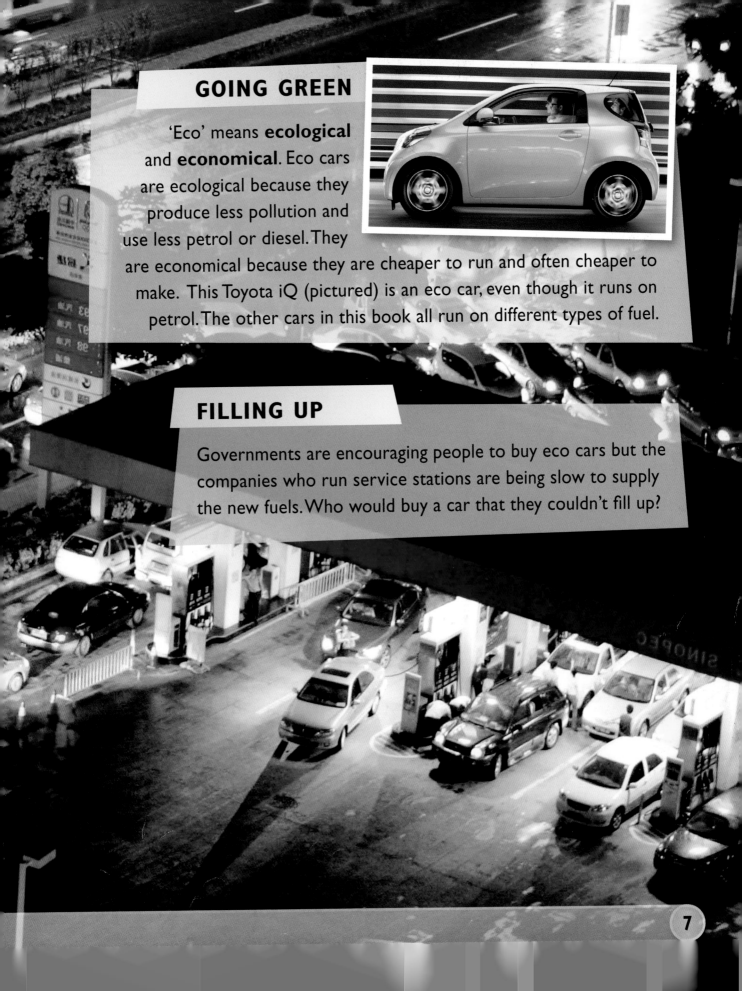

GOING GREEN

'Eco' means **ecological** and **economical**. Eco cars are ecological because they produce less pollution and use less petrol or diesel. They are economical because they are cheaper to run and often cheaper to make. This Toyota iQ (pictured) is an eco car, even though it runs on petrol. The other cars in this book all run on different types of fuel.

FILLING UP

Governments are encouraging people to buy eco cars but the companies who run service stations are being slow to supply the new fuels. Who would buy a car that they couldn't fill up?

TOYOTA PRIUS

The Toyota Prius has secured a place in car history. It was the first **hybrid** car to go into production. Since its launch in 1997, Toyota has sold over 1.2 million cars and they are improving its technology all the time. A hybrid is a car that runs on more than one type of fuel.

HYBRID

The Prius is powered by both petrol and electricity. The petrol engine is small because the electric motor can give the car the extra power it needs. The electric motor is charged by the petrol engine when driving along. This means the Prius uses less petrol than other cars – it can go 100 km on almost 4 litres of petrol or over 70 miles on one gallon.

STATS AND FACTS

- **Top speed:** 177 km/h (110 mph)
- **CO$_2$ emissions:** 89 g/km
- **Country of origin:** Japan
- **Cost:** from £18,000
- **Claim to fame:** A hybrid family car – less petrol, lower CO$_2$.

CLIMATE CHANGE

Scientists tell us that too much carbon dioxide in the air is causing our climate to change. It is one of the 'greenhouse gases' that trap in the sun's heat, just as a greenhouse does. This is causing global warming.

CO$_2$ EMISSIONS

Carbon dioxide, or CO$_2$, is a gas. It is what is left over when petrol and diesel are burned. The CO$_2$ comes out of the **exhaust pipe** at the back of a car and goes into the air. With all the cars, trucks, buses and motorbikes in the world, that's a lot of gas! But when the Prius is running on electricity, it produces no CO$_2$.

LEXUS GS 450H

The Lexus GS 450h is a hybrid car that has the looks of a luxury car and the performance to match. It has a smaller engine than similar cars but it has a high-powered electric motor as well. Working together, the car performs like similar cars but burns less fuel and pumps out less CO_2.

GOOD LOOKS

Many eco cars are small. Sometimes they are ugly. And to get real **fuel efficiency** you need to drive them slowly. None of this is true of the Lexus GS 450h.

STATS AND FACTS

- **Top speed:** 250 km/h (155 mph)
- **CO$_2$ emissions:** 185 g/km
- **Country of origin:** Japan
- **Cost:** from £40,000
- **Claim to fame:** A high-performing hybrid – less petrol, lower CO$_2$.

SMOOTH AND SILENT

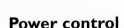

When you press the start button of a Lexus GS 450h the lights go on but there is no sound. The petrol engine isn't needed.
It is the silent electric motor that's in charge.
It even provides the power to pull away.

The petrol engine fires up when more power is needed. Lexus have made the switch from electric motor to petrol engine so smooth it is hardly noticeable.

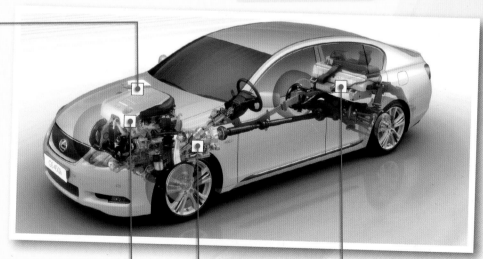

Power control

Hybrid transmission

High output N-MH battery

Petrol engine

TESLA ROADSTER

The Tesla Roadster looks like a sports car and is as fast as a sports car. However, it needs no petrol, makes no noise and gives off no CO_2. It runs entirely on electricity – clean, instant power. Plug it in when you get home, charge it up and off you go again.

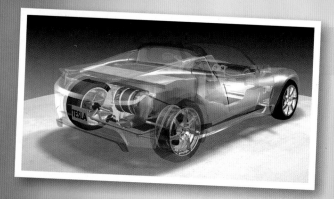

LOTUS PLUS

The Tesla Roadster begins life as a Lotus Elise **fibreglass** body. Then American company Tesla takes over. Instead of an engine, they put in 6,831 batteries.

It costs just £3.50 to charge the batteries, compared to almost £40 to fill a Lotus Elise with petrol. BUT, the Tesla costs three times more!

CHARGE TO THE FINISH

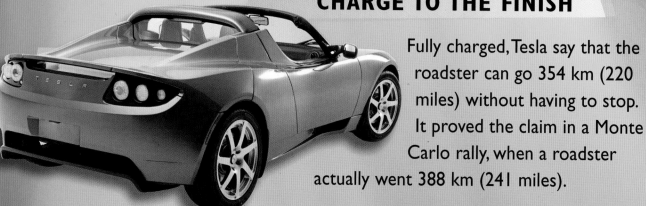

Fully charged, Tesla say that the roadster can go 354 km (220 miles) without having to stop. It proved the claim in a Monte Carlo rally, when a roadster actually went 388 km (241 miles).

STATS AND FACTS

- **Top speed:** 201 km/h (125 mph)
- **CO_2 emissions:** 0 g/km
- **Country of origin:** USA
- **Cost:** from £87,000
- **Claim to fame:** A plug-in electric sports car – high performance, no petrol, no CO_2.

THE GOOD AND THE BAD

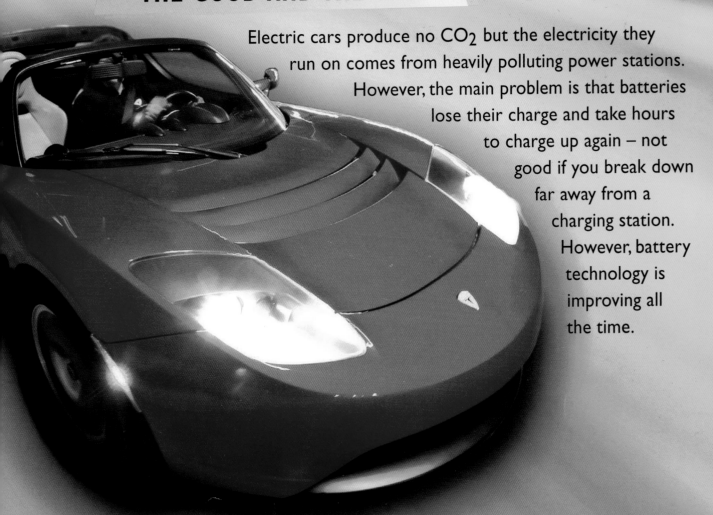

Electric cars produce no CO_2 but the electricity they run on comes from heavily polluting power stations. However, the main problem is that batteries lose their charge and take hours to charge up again – not good if you break down far away from a charging station. However, battery technology is improving all the time.

LIGHTNING GT

With its head-turning supercar looks, the Lightning GT wouldn't look out of place beside an Aston Martin or a Maserati. The difference is that, when it hits the roads, it will be the first electric supercar. It is very beautiful, but only costs 1.37p a kilometre to run.

BRILLIANT BATTERIES

The Lightning team are using special batteries in their GT. The batteries should have a longer life than other electric car batteries. Also, they can be charged almost as quickly as it takes to fill up a large **4x4**.

REGENERATIVE BRAKING

When you ride a bike, you pedal fast to pick up speed. When you brake, all the energy you used to get the wheels going is lost. The same happens in a car, but the lost energy means wasted fuel. What the Lightning GT does is reverse the motor so the energy is put back into the battery – so braking actually generates electricity.

STATS AND FACTS

- **Top speed:** limited to 130 mph (205 km/h)
- **CO_2 emissions:** 0 g/km
- **Country of origin:** UK
- **Cost:** from £120,000
- **Claim to fame:** A plug-in electric supercar – superfast charge time, no petrol, no CO_2.

WHEEL POWER

In many electric and hybrid cars, the battery packs and motors add weight to the car. Moving this extra weight requires more power. Not so with the Lightning GT. The four lightweight electric motors are in the wheels.

HONDA CIVIC GX NGV

Honda is a world leader in eco car development. They have produced hybrids, electric cars and this – the Civic GX. It runs on compressed natural gas (CNG). CNG is safer, cheaper and greener than petrol or diesel, and you can fill up at home for about £5.

CLEAN AIR

In the busy city of New Delhi in India, CNG is making a real difference. The heavy-polluting rickshaws (little taxis) now run on CNG. The air in New Delhi is now much cleaner, and it is a nicer place to live and work. Other cities have CNG buses and postal vans.

ADAPTABLE ENGINE

The Civic GX looks like an ordinary Honda Civic. The engine is the same as an ordinary Civic's, but instead of burning petrol or diesel it burns natural gas. Instead of a petrol tank, it has a gas storage tank at the back of the car.

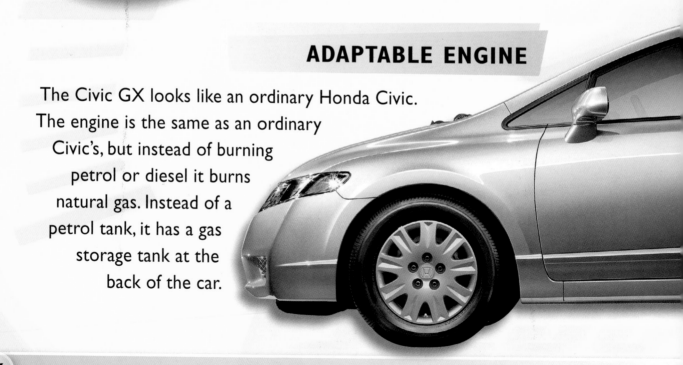

STATS AND FACTS

- **Top speed:** 185 km/h (115 mph)
- **CO_2 emissions:** under 1 g/km
- **Country of origin:** Japan
- **Cost:** from £16,000
- **Claim to fame:** A family car that runs on CNG – cheap, safe fuel, hardly any CO_2, no petrol.

FILL IT UP

Natural gas is used for cooking and heating in many homes. You can fill up your car from the same supply if you have a special box fitted, but filling up can take all night. In some countries there are fast-fill pumps in service stations. However, there is not an endless supply of gas, so it is not a real solution to the world's energy problems.

BMW HYDROGEN SEVEN

Like Honda, BMW are world leaders in efficient motoring and new car technology. Many of their cars already have eco features, but their Hydrogen Seven goes one step further. As well as petrol, it can run on **liquid hydrogen**, and the only thing to come out of the engine is **water vapour**.

HYDROGEN

Hydrogen is the most plentiful gas in the universe. It is so light that it sits high above Earth's **atmosphere**, but when it mixes with **oxygen**, it makes water. We have plenty of that on Earth, so all the clever scientists do is take the hydrogen from water. Then they turn it into a liquid fuel.

DUAL FUEL

The Hydrogen Seven has two fuel tanks. One tank holds enough hydrogen to go 201 km (125 miles). The other holds enough petrol to go 482 km (300 miles). The driver chooses which fuel to use with no loss of power or performance, but **fuel consumption** is high.

STATS AND FACTS

- **Top speed:** limited to 230 km/h (143 mph)
- **CO_2 emissions:** 0 g/km (in hydrogen mode)
- **Country of origin:** Germany
- **Cost:** Not yet available to buy
- **Claim to fame:** A luxury car that can run on liquid hydrogen, which produces no CO_2.

THE GOOD AND THE BAD

BMW believe that hydrogen could be the future of motoring. Many agree, but turning hydrogen from a gas to a liquid costs a lot and uses a huge amount of electricity. If that electricity came from wind, solar or wave power, it would be truly eco-friendly. Right now, very little does.

HONDA FCX CLARITY

The Honda FCX Clarity is one of the most advanced cars in the world. It has **hydrogen fuel-cell technology**. Honda have only produced a few cars so far. They are being driven by famous test drivers in California in the USA. That is one of the only places in the world where you can fill up with hydrogen gas.

HOW IT WORKS

It's very clever science. What the car does is produce its own electricity. It does this by mixing hydrogen gas, stored in a tank in the car, with oxygen in the air to make electricity and water. The electricity powers the car's motor and the harmless water is released into the air.

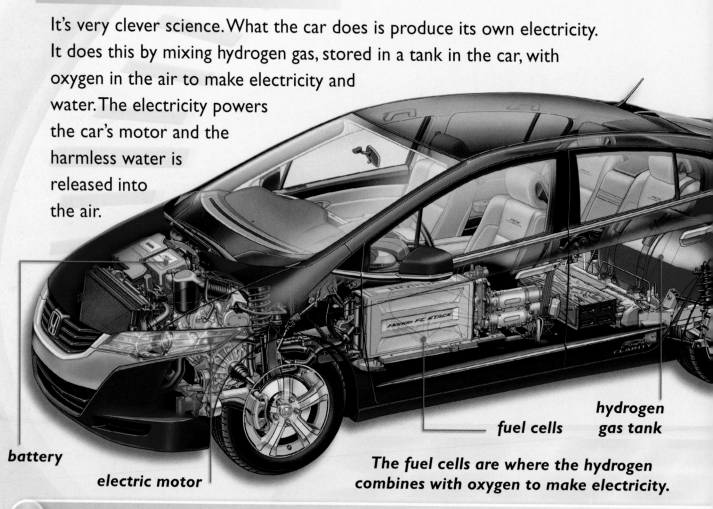

battery

electric motor

fuel cells

hydrogen gas tank

The fuel cells are where the hydrogen combines with oxygen to make electricity.

- **Top speed:** 161 km/h (100 mph)
- **CO_2 emissions:** 0 g/km
- **Country of origin:** Japan
- **Cost:** Not yet available to buy
- **Claim to fame:** A family car that turns hydrogen gas into electricity. No plug-in. No petrol. No CO_2.

HONDA FC SPORT

Honda has been learning important lessons about fuel cell technology since it released its first **prototypes** in 1999. Over time the fuel cells have become smaller and lighter. They are developing this FC sport – a supercar with fuel cell technology.

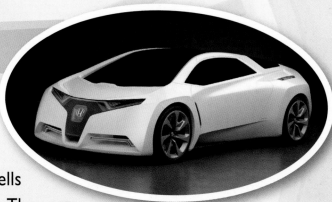

FILLING UP

Honda are working on ways to expand the number of places drivers can go to fill up with hydrogen. They are also working on a home energy station. This could be developed to provide electricity to power your house as well as your car.

SAAB 9-5 BIOPOWER

Swedish company Saab have introduced 'biopower' cars. These are **flex-fuel** vehicles that can run on **bioethanol**, a mix of petrol and ethanol, made from plants such as sugar and corn. Burning **ethanol** does produce CO_2, but the crops grown to make it also absorb CO_2 from the air. So biopower pollutes, but then it cleans it up!

BIOPOWER

Saab's biopower range is only sold in countries where **biofuels** are easily available and cheap. In countries like Britain, bioethanol can only be bought at a few petrol stations, so those wanting a Saab 9-5 have to buy a petrol or diesel model.

STATS AND FACTS

- **Top speed:** 225 km/h (140 mph)
- **CO$_2$ emissions:** 204 g/km
- **Country of origin:** Sweden
- **Cost:** from £16,770
- **Claim to fame:** A luxury car that runs on a biofuel made from plants – an eco alternative to petrol.

CORN FUEL

Biofuels include ethanol and **biodiesel**, both made from plant or animal matter, such as corn and cow poo! Biofuels have a big advantage over oil. Once oil is burned, it is gone. Plants can be grown and harvested every year. However, some people argue that biofuels are not eco-friendly at all because farmers use polluting chemicals and fuel to produce the crops.

MIX IT UP

In Thailand, as in other countries, the fuel you buy is already mixed with a *little* biofuel. The Saab engine, however, can run on fuel that is *mostly* ethanol. This makes a little bit of petrol go a long way.

FIAT SIENA TETRAFUEL

The Fiat Siena Tetrafuel is the ultimate flex-fuel vehicle. It can run on four types of fuel – ethanol, compressed natural gas (CNG), petrol and an ethanol/petrol mix. It's not the most beautiful car in this book, but it is cheap and extremely clever. It decides which fuel will be the most efficient to use as you drive.

Some worry that if farmers switch to growing crops to make ethanol, less food will be produced.

BIO BRAZIL

Fiat have only launched the Siena in Brazil and Argentina, where flex-fuel vehicles are common. Brazil grows lots of sugar (pictured) and they are using it to make cheap ethanol. Soon, Brazilian petrol stations might become known as 'ethanol stations'.

STATS AND FACTS

- **Top speed:** approx 156 km/h (97 mph)
- **CO$_2$ emissions:** varies, depending on fuel used
- **Country of origin:** Brazil
- **Cost:** from £10,000
- **Claim to fame:** A cheap car that can run on four types of fuel, including cheap eco alternatives to petrol.

CLEVER CAR

The Siena's on-board computer switches between the different fuels without the driver noticing. It burns the liquid fuel for accelerating and high-speed driving. It switches to gas for slow, city driving. If you run out of one, it will use the other.

Here are the gas tanks in the boot for the CNG.

NOVO SIENA

TWO TANKS

Like some other hybrids, the Siena has two types of fuel tank. One is for the liquids – the ethanol or petrol or petrol mix. You can fill this tank up with whatever is available or cheap. The other is for the gas.

WORLDFIRST RACING CAR

Not only does this car run on plants, it's also made from them! It has a steering wheel made from carrots, wing mirrors made from potato starch and a body made from recycled materials. It is a prototype, built by scientists at the University of Warwick in the UK.

CHOCOLATE FUEL

The engine is a BMW turbo diesel engine that has been altered to run on biodiesel. According to the team who made this car, 'Anything with a fat in it can be turned into diesel.' Even chocolate! Cocoa beans, from which chocolate is made, contain a lot of fat.

HIGH PERFORMANCE

The team has used the most advanced technology to build this high-performance racing car. They will share what they learn with other universities and companies. This could pave the way to making motor racing a greener sport.

STATS AND FACTS

- **Top speed:** 241 km/h (150 mph)
- **CO$_2$ emissions:** not known
- **Country of origin:** UK
- **Cost:** £200,000
- **Claim to fame:** The world's first racing car made from and run on plants.

FIBRE BODY

When carrots are made into carrot juice, a **pulp** is left over. This is what the steering wheel is made from. The body is partly made from a crop called flax. Flax is blended with recycled **carbon-fibre** to make the body very strong.

GLOSSARY

4x4 a short name for a four-wheel drive vehicle, where the engine powers all four wheels at the same time, not just two as on normal cars

atmosphere the air and other gases that surround the Earth

biodiesel a fuel for diesel engines made from plant oils and animal fats

bioethanol a fuel that is a replacement for petrol made from crops like wheat, corn, sugarbeet or sugar cane

biofuels fuels like bioethanol and biodiesel that are made from plant and animal matter and will not run out.

carbon-dioxide emissions carbon dioxide is a gas that scientists tell us is harming our environment. It is given off (or emitted) from cars when they burn petrol or diesel.

carbon-fibre a material made of little strings of carbon, a substance even stronger than metal

CO$_2$ a short name for carbon dioxide

ecological when something is good for, or causes less damage to, our environment

economical when something is not wasteful – it uses the minimum needed and does not waste money

emission something that is given off (emitted) such as gases coming from a car or light coming from the sun

ethanol a type of alcohol made from plants

exhaust pipe the part of a

car where waste gases from the engine are released into the air

fibreglass a hard, flexible material made from tiny fibres of glass

flex-fuel can run on more than one type of fuel

fuel consumption how much fuel a car uses, usually measured by how many litres a car uses to go 100 km (or how many miles it can go on one gallon)

fuel efficiency burning as little fuel as possible

global warming an increase in temperatures around the world said to be caused by greenhouse gases, which includes CO_2.

hybrid something that is a cross between two different things, eg. a petrol-driven car and an electric car

hydrogen fuel-cell technology a new way to generate power when hydrogen is mixed with oxygen to create electricity and water

liquid hydrogen hydrogen gas that has been turned into a liquid

oxygen a type of gas which is needed by all living things to survive

pollutants things that pollute, for example weedkiller and tractors

prototype a product made and used for testing before others are made, to see if it works and how to improve it

pulp the soft, moist stuff left behind after juice has been squeezed out of a plant or vegetable, such as a carrot or orange.

technology the use of science and the latest equipment

water vapour water that has turned into a gas in the air, usually because it has been heated up

INDEX